TRAVIS KELCE

Making a Difference Beyond Football

By Katie Kawa

People Who Make a Difference

Published in 2026 by
KidHaven Publishing, an Imprint of Greenhaven Publishing, LLC
2544 Clinton St.
Buffalo, NY 14224

Designer: Deanna Lepovich
Editor: Katie Kawa

Photo credits: Cover Cal Sport Media/Alamy Stock Photo; pp. 5, 9, 20 Ringo Chiu/Shutterstock.com; pp. 7, 15 (main and inset) UPI/Alamy Stock Photo; p. 11 Sipa USA/Alamy Stock Photo; p. 13 Dean R Specker/Shutterstock.com; p. 17 Featureflash Photo Agency/Shutterstock.com; p. 19 Jamie Lamor Thompson/Shutterstock.com; p. 21 T.Sumaetho/Shutterstock.com.

Cataloging-in-Publication Data

Names: Kawa, Katie.
Title: Travis Kelce: making a difference beyond football / Katie Kawa.
Description: Buffalo, NY : KidHaven Publishing, 2026. | Series: People who make a difference | Includes glossary and index.
Identifiers: ISBN 9781534549555 (pbk.) | ISBN 9781534549562 (library bound) | ISBN 9781534549579 (ebook)
Subjects: LCSH: Kelce, Travis, 1989–Juvenile literature. | Kansas City Chiefs (Football team)–Juvenile literature. | Tight ends (Football)–United States–Biography–Juvenile literature. | Football players–United States–Biography–Juvenile literature.
Classification: LCC GV939.K36 K39 2026 | DDC 796.332092–dc23

Printed in the United States of America

CPSIA compliance information: Batch #CSKH26: For further information contact Greenhaven Publishing LLC at 1-844-317-7404.

CONTENTS

A TEAM PLAYER

Travis Kelce knows what it takes to be part of a successful team. He's won multiple Super Bowls with the Kansas City Chiefs, which means he's been part of the best team in the National Football League (NFL) more than once. Travis uses his skills as a tight end to help the Chiefs win games, and he also works hard to be a good teammate in practice and after both wins and losses.

Travis is a team player outside of football too. He does what he can to help the people around him succeed—from his family members to kids in his community.

In His Words

"I just want to be known as one of the best teammates these guys [his fellow Chiefs] have ever had."

— Interview before Super Bowl LIX in February 2025

Travis's ability to make a difference beyond football was highlighted when he was nominated for the Walter Payton NFL Man of the Year Award in 2020 and 2024. This meant he was a finalist for this honor, which is given to a player who's known for helping his community.

GROWING UP IN OHIO

Travis Kelce was born near Cleveland, Ohio, on October 5, 1989. He grew up in Cleveland Heights with his parents, Ed and Donna, and his older brother, Jason. Jason and Travis played many sports as kids, such as football, baseball, and basketball, but football is where they found the most success.

Travis played quarterback in high school, which means his job was to throw the ball to his teammates. However, he mostly played tight end after high school. A tight end catches passes from the quarterback and blocks the other team's players so they don't tackle his teammates.

In His Words

"Growing up in Cleveland Heights with supportive family and friends, I know the power of having people in your corner."

— Interview after being nominated for the Walter Payton NFL Man of the Year Award in December 2024

Travis and Jason are shown here when they played against each other in the Super Bowl in 2023. The brothers are very close. Travis even followed in Jason's footsteps and went to college at the University of Cincinnati, where they both played football.

CHOSEN AS A CHIEF

Travis was drafted, or chosen, by the Kansas City Chiefs in the third round of the 2013 NFL draft. Travis's new coach was Andy Reid, who had also coached Jason when they were both with the Philadelphia Eagles. Andy talked to Jason about Travis before deciding to draft him.

Travis spent most of the 2013 season injured, or hurt, so he only played in one game. He started to have more success on the field in 2014, and in 2015, he was chosen to go to the Pro Bowl, which is a game featuring the best players in the NFL.

In His Words

"I'm going to be who I am. That's what's gotten me here."

— Interview with *Sports Illustrated* magazine from October 2017

Travis went from being the 63rd pick in the NFL draft to being one of the league's best and most famous players!

BECOMING A CHAMPION

At the beginning of 2016, Travis played in his first **playoff** game with the Chiefs. However, there was still a missing piece that needed to be found before the team could become a Super Bowl **champion**. That missing piece was quarterback Patrick Mahomes, who was drafted by the Chiefs in 2017 and became their starting quarterback in 2018.

Patrick quickly became one of the best quarterbacks in the NFL, and he and Travis worked well together. In 2020, they won their first Super Bowl by beating the San Francisco 49ers. Travis scored a touchdown in the game!

In His Words

"I love what I do and I love doing it with the people that ... I do it with."

— Interview with *CBS Mornings* from September 2024

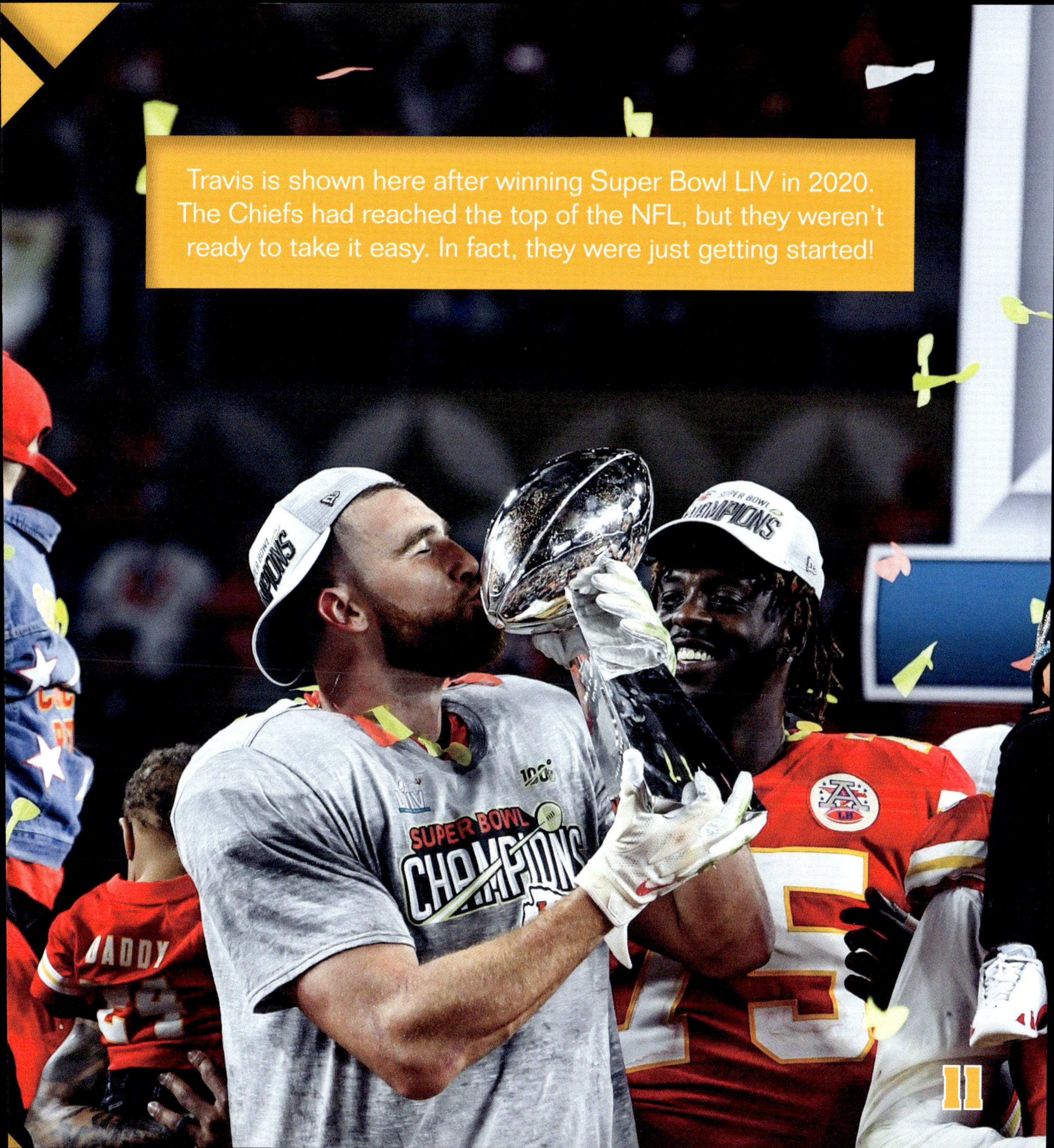

Travis is shown here after winning Super Bowl LIV in 2020. The Chiefs had reached the top of the NFL, but they weren't ready to take it easy. In fact, they were just getting started!

BACK TO THE BIG GAME

Travis made it back to the Super Bowl in 2021, but the Chiefs lost to the Tampa Bay Buccaneers. Then, in 2023, the Chiefs played the Eagles in Super Bowl LVII. This meant that Travis played against Jason! In the battle between the brothers, Travis was the winner—the Chiefs beat the Eagles to win another Super Bowl.

The Chiefs faced the 49ers in the Super Bowl once again in 2024, and just like in 2020, they won the game. However, the next year, their winning **streak** ended when they lost to the Eagles in Super Bowl LIX.

In His Words

"I used to want to be known as the greatest tight end ever. I think [now] it's just more so enjoying these moments that I have with my teammates and trying to get these wins and create these memories."

— Interview before Super Bowl LIX in February 2025

Travis is shown here with Chiefs fans after winning the Super Bowl in 2024. That year, Travis broke the NFL record for most passes caught in the playoffs, with 165. He also holds the NFL record for most playoff touchdowns scored by a tight end.

WORKING WITH JASON

Travis's success on the field made him famous among football fans. However, he reached new heights of fame thanks to the podcast he hosts with his brother, called *New Heights*. They began recording the show, where they talk about their lives, the NFL, and anything else that's on their minds, in 2022. It's become a huge hit!

Travis and Jason also appeared in a **documentary** called *Kelce*, which came out in 2023. It mainly followed Jason during the 2022 NFL season. However, Travis played an important part in it, because that was when the brothers faced each other in the Super Bowl.

In His Words

"I'm forever grateful [thankful] for who my brother is in my life. He's always been the guy that I can kind of just lean on."

— Interview with *CBS Mornings* from September 2024

Travis is known for supporting the people he loves, such as parents, his brother, and the music superstar Taylor Swift, who he began dating in 2023.

A HELPING HAND

Travis has become one of the NFL's biggest stars. He's appeared on TV shows such as *Saturday Night Live*, in **commercials**, and on the covers of magazines. However, he hasn't forgotten where he came from.

In 2015, Travis started 87 and Running to give young people, especially those in Cleveland Heights, a chance to succeed. This **foundation** also helps young people in Kansas City, Missouri. It provides money for educational **programs** in these communities. In addition, 87 and Running is giving money to the University of Cincinnati to support the **mental** health of students who play sports at the school.

In His Words

"Being able to give back to the community here in Kansas City as well as show love to my hometown is not something I'll ever take for granted."

— Interview after being nominated for the Walter Payton NFL Man of the Year Award in December 2024

Travis started 87 and Running because he believes that all kids should be given the same opportunities to learn, grow, and find success that he had when he was younger. It's named after the number Travis wears for the Chiefs.

IN THE LAB

In Kansas City, 87 and Running teamed up with a group called Operation Breakthrough to help kids from **underserved** communities before school, after school, and during the summer. Operation Breakthrough gives kids a safe place to learn, play, eat, and receive health care while their parents are at work. Travis believes in what this group is doing and has helped in many different ways.

One of the biggest ways Travis has helped Operation Breakthrough is by providing money and support for the Ignition Lab. This is a space for teenagers to go after school to learn more about STEM, business, and life skills.

In His Words

"I think we need to stand up and make a change and make a difference in our communities."

— Interview with SiriusXM NFL Radio from August 2020

The Life of Travis Kelce

1989
Travis Kelce is born in Ohio on October 5.

2008
Travis starts school at the University of Cincinnati.

2013
The Kansas City Chiefs select Travis with the 63rd pick in the NFL draft.

2015
Travis is chosen to play in his first Pro Bowl and starts his foundation, 87 and Running.

2016
Travis plays in his first NFL playoff game.

2020
Travis is nominated for the Walter Payton NFL Man of the Year Award and wins his first Super Bowl.

2021
Travis and his teammates lose to the Tampa Bay Buccaneers in the Super Bowl.

2022
Travis and his brother, Jason, start a podcast called *New Heights*.

2023
Travis wins his second Super Bowl, appears in *Kelce*, hosts *Saturday Night Live*, and begins dating Taylor Swift.

2024
The Chiefs beat the San Francisco 49ers to win the Super Bowl, and Travis breaks the NFL record for most passes caught in the playoffs.

2025
Travis and the rest of the Chiefs lose to the Philadelphia Eagles in the Super Bowl.

Travis Kelce has had a very long and successful NFL **career**, featuring many trips to the Super Bowl!

WORKING WITH OTHERS

It takes all kinds of people to have a winning team. Travis knows this, and that's why he's often spoken about the importance of accepting and respecting all people. He's called attention to the problem of **racism** in the United States and has spoken to students about this issue.

A good teammate supports the people around him and works to help others succeed. This is what Travis Kelce has done—and continues to do—as a part of the Kansas City Chiefs and a part of his community. He believes that making a real difference isn't done by scoring touchdowns. It's done by helping others.

In His Words

"I think I found it all. I just gotta [have to] ... keep it all. I absolutely love where I am in life."

— Interview with Westwood One Sports from February 2025

Be Like Travis Kelce!

Support your friends and family. You can do this by telling them you love and care about them, helping them with chores and other tasks, or taking time to play with or talk to them.

Work hard in school and in whatever activities you do, such as dance classes, sports, or music lessons.

If you are on a team or part of a club, be a good teammate! Treat everyone in the group with respect, work hard to help everyone succeed, and listen when someone is having a hard time.

Talk to others about causes you care about and things that matter to you.

Learn more about issues such as racism.

Raise money for groups that help people with their mental health.

Raise money for groups that help kids in underserved communities.

You don't have to be a great football player to be like Travis Kelce. You can start by doing your part to help others.

GLOSSARY

career: A period of time spent doing a job or activity.

champion: A winner of a championship—a contest to find out who is the best player or team in a sport.

commercial: A short clip shown on TV that is created to make people want to buy a good or service.

documentary: A nonfiction movie or television program presenting facts about a topic.

foundation: A group supported by money from one or more people with the purpose of helping others.

mental: Relating to the mind.

playoff: One of a series of games played after the regular season of a sport is over to find out who the best team is that season.

program: A set of classes or events related to a certain subject.

racism: The practice of treating others poorly because they are part of a different race, or group of people who look alike in certain ways.

streak: A period or series, especially in sports.

underserved: Not given access to certain important services, such as health and social services.

FOR MORE INFORMATION

WEBSITES

87 and Running

87running.org

The official website of Travis's foundation offers facts about how it helps young people in Kansas City, Cleveland Heights, and Cincinnati.

Travis Kelce

www.chiefs.com/team/players-roster/travis-kelce/

Travis's page on the website for the Kansas City Chiefs features many facts about his NFL career.

BOOKS

Adamson, Thomas K. *Travis Kelce*. Minneapolis, MN: Bellwether Media, 2025.

Stabler, David. *Meet Travis Kelce*. Minneapolis, MN: Lerner Publications, 2024.

Van Cleave, Ryan G. *Travis Kelce: Superstar Tight End*. North Mankato, MN: Capstone Press, 2025.

INDEX